CREATING THE NORTH HIGHLAND WAY

About the author

Tina Irving is a businesswoman with many years of experience as a project manager in financial services. She has lived and worked in Scotland in the tourism for 15 years both as a consultant to the owner of the bed & breakfast, tearoom and campsite on Dunnet Head. She also has a wide experience of tourism in Spain and has recently launched LetsGoSouth meets LetsGoNorth, a collaboration of businesses dedicated to developing rural tourism in both Scotland and southern Spain where she has had businesses and property for over 30 years.

Tina is a graduate of London South Bank and Heriot Watt Universities. In the first instance, she has a degree in Computing and Spanish, and in the second instance a Post Graduate Diploma in Environmental Economics, Policy and Risk. In 2003, launched the Dunnet Head Educational Trust to raise the profile of Dunnet Head as the most northerly point of the UK mainland. When she moved to Caithness in 2000 she immediately saw the potential of the Head and that it was not marketed as its near neighbour John o Groats is. Dunnet Head is the focal point of the North Highland Way as all of the administration and promotion have been done from there.

Tina is also an Associate Researcher at London South Bank University and as an ex alumni monitors students from the

© 2015 Brough Bay Ltd.
All Rights Reserved

University. She is also a member of the National Union of Journalists.

Copyright

The copyright is that of Brough Bay Ltd. Registered in England. Company No. 06638448

Executive Summary

This document was written by a freelance journalist once the management company LetsGoNorth abandoned the North Highland Way project after making an investment of £30,000 in time, office services and project management. The feasibility study and business plan are for sale on the web site of Christian Hart, Glasgow. The project was handed over to the Dunnet Head Educational Trust, a social enterprise, and funding for coordination was applied for to Foundation Scotland. There is some doubt that they even assessed the application. The Trust also applied to the Communities Fund monitored by Dounreay on two occasions and were rejected.

The document is backed by emails, letters and other materials and can be completely verified. The management company charges a fee of £15 per retrieval and they are protected by copyright. Many of them are available on the web site at www.letsgonorthnewsservice.com – cost £15 to access them.

© 2015 Brough Bay Ltd.
All Rights Reserved

Funds are reinvested in the development of the Way.

History

The North Highland Way was first mooted by the Caithness Waybaggers in 1992 and had been talked about in tourism circles for many years. In 2013 launched the North Highland Way with eight local businessmen. The number quickly grew to over forty, including Easyways, a Falkirk based walking company who sponsored the waymarkers. The North Highland Way talked about by the Caithness Waybaggers took a different route from Dunbeath to the north coast and then to John o Groats.

What is the North Highland Way

The North Highland Way is a coastal route from John o Groats to Cape Wrath, and any route within 10 miles of the coast. It is not envisaged as a built path, but more of a "way to go". The route can be used by any users under the Land Reform (Scotland) Act 2003. It is not intended for any motor driven vehicle.

The aim of the project is to attend to the gaps in provision of the Core Path Plans which are the responsibility of the Highland Council. The Core Path Plan maps can be seen on the Highland Council web site.

© 2015 Brough Bay Ltd.
All Rights Reserved

Why the North Highland Way

The North Highland Way could bring economic and social development to the far flung corner of Scotland and all across the coast. Given the resources, the Way could create jobs, attract new businesses to the area, and generally encourage inward investment. The tourism product in Scotland is fragmented at best. The problem is magnified in the far north where population is low and businesses and public services do not work together. In short, there is too much emphasis on the voluntary sector.

What is the vision for the national trail

The vision is for the route from John o Groats to Cape Wrath, and to include trails 10 miles inland, which would become part of the Scottish National Trail which is a vision for many. The route would be suitable for all non motorised vehicles as under the terms of the Land Reform (Scotland) Act 2003.

This model was used when developing the Moray Firth Trail along the Moray and East coast of Sutherland to John o Groats. The Cape Wrath Trail was launched in 2012 and there is clearly interest in creating long distance trails, but not built paths. The North Highland Way was designed to link the two existing routes.

© 2015 Brough Bay Ltd.
All Rights Reserved

Funding

The vision is somewhat of an idealistic view as the Highland Council are responsible for the Core Path Networks under the said Land Reform Act and there are several problems of maintenance and upkeep even on the Core Paths. These are identified in the feasibility study and business plan which is available for sale separately. There also difficulties caused by land funded by HIE. Neither HIE nor the Highland Council want to fund the project, or even have an input to its development. There have been several attempts at engagement but it has all come to naught at the time of writing as they want everything done on a voluntary basis. Dounreay have refused funding twice and Foundation Scotland once. The writer would direct the reader to those organisations as to why funding has been refused. It is not to say it will not be granted in the future.

The writer has approached Holyrood direct to see if there might be other options rather than the standard voluntary sector method which is time consuming and totally impractical given the resources available.

Resources required

As with any other project, resources are required. These are traditionally defined as land, labour and money. The writer

© 2015 Brough Bay Ltd.
All Rights Reserved

also includes time in the equation. The old addage time=money certainly applies – a fact which escapes the Highland Council who want the project to be delivered as a community project. This is just not possible. They have no resources. Members of community councils typically have jobs (where they earn income), busy family lives and other commitments which may take precedence over the development of the Way. A dedicated coordinator is required – ie labour. The community councils have no money. The Highland Council have reduced their budgets in 2014 for the third year in a row. The community councils are understandably focussed on their own communities all of which have different priorities. Playgrounds, examining planning requests and maintenance of their own areas may be more important to them than developing a national trail. Some of the expertise inherent in these community councils is phenomenal and of course local knowledge of trails is second to none. However, how will all of this information be captured without labour and therefore money?

The company Brough Bay Ltd. T/a LetsGoNorth first took up the mantle of the Way on a commercial basis. The businesses were delighted and happy to support financially as they felt the return on investment would be high. For some such as the Ben Loyal Hotel, Weavers cafe and the Wild Orchid return has been good.

Coordination is key to the project. The Company Brough Bay

© 2015 Brough Bay Ltd.
All Rights Reserved

Ltd. Started off by managing the project and coordinating it until it became too expensive in time, travel and office costs. It has since been passed to the Dunnet Head Educational Trust and they have formed Friends of the North Highland Way.

Robust community consultation – in addition to that carried out by the Highland Council as described at Annex A.

Feasibility study
Business plan
Land owner consultation

© 2015 Brough Bay Ltd.
All Rights Reserved

Marketing

Robust marketing has been carried out. Exhibitions at the Scrabster ferry port and Inverness and Wick airports have been held.

Google Analytics on the web site, Facebook and Twitter pages.

Web site firstly as part of the web site at www.letsgonorth.com, then there were some technical difficulties which had to be overcome and a new web site launched.

Since October 2014, LetsGoNorth have been marketing the Way in Spain under the LetsGoNorth meets LetsGoSouth project – http://www.letsgosouth.co.uk.

A challenge event has been set up for 2015 and is being marketed on www.dunnethead.co.uk

Advertising

Scottish Walks
Active Magazine published by Scottish Provincial Press (twice)

Potential Partners

© 2015 Brough Bay Ltd.
All Rights Reserved

Private Sector
	Dounreay – feasibility study includes emails and letters from the fund holders
	Participating businesses

		Natural Retreats, John o Groats
		Seaview Hotel, John o Groats
		John o Groats Caravanning and Campsite
		Dunnet Head B&B, campsite and tearooms
		Lau-ren House, Barrock
		Sandra's Backpackers, Thurso
		Holborn Hotel, Thurso
		Pentland Self Catering Cottages, Thurso
		Weigh Inn, Thurso
		Pennyland Hotel, Thurso
		Marine B&B, Thurso
		Angela Morris, Thurso
		Old Mill, Reay
		Halladale Inn, Melvich
		Betty Hill Cafe, Betty Hill
		Sharvedda B&B, Strathy
		Cloisters B&B, Melness
		Weavers Cafe, Tongue
		Ben Loyal Hotel, Tongue
		Wild Orchid Guest House, Durness
		White Heather Cafe, Durness
		Easyways Walking Company
		Durness Bus

© 2015 Brough Bay Ltd.
All Rights Reserved

Bobby's Buses

Legalities
    Land Reform (Scotland) Act 2003
    Scottish Outdoor Access Code

What are the obstacles
    Public services (except for SNH)
    Attitude of some sectors of the community
    Lack of understanding of economics and business both in the community and of public services
    Too much reliance on voluntary sector

History

The North Highland Way was first mooted by the local group the Caithness Waybaggers in 1992 and was spoken about many times in tourism meetings in the far north of Scotland. Development of the walking product in general is on the agenda of the Highland Council and has been identified as being of importance at charettes in Wick and Thurso. The development of the Way is now on the Caithness & Sutherland Local Plan.

The group of eight businessmen soon grew to nearly forty, waymarkers were sponsored by the walking company, EasyWays, and the Friends of the North Highland Way was

© 2015 Brough Bay Ltd.
All Rights Reserved

formed in 2014 under the auspices of the Dunnet Head Educational Trust, a social enterprise, based at the focal point of the Way, Dunnet Head, which is the most northerly point of the UK mainland.

Structure

The Way has never been mooted as a built trail, a point made clear from the outset to public services. A built trail would simply be too expensive. The facilities envisaged were as those of the South West Coastal Path or the Welsh Coastal Path which are built paths, but have a wealth of facilities in the form of cycle hire, accommodation provision, cafes, restaurants and outdoor activity centres and retail. The benefits are for all.

LetsGoNorth poured money into the project. The phone bills were horrendous, at over £100 per month for the eight months of the start up. The management time charged at a project manager hourly rate of a conservative £40 per hour reached £15000 before the management company pulled out and the Friends of the North Highland Way was developed in an attempt to raise much needed revenue.

A magazine was relaunched – the North Highland Explorer – to support the project and all of the contributors to the Way. The quarterly magazine is now available on subscription on line at www.letsgonorth.com.

© 2015 Brough Bay Ltd.
All Rights Reserved

LetsGoNorth formed alliances with organisations such as Walking World, which promotes walking to a database of 60,000 walkers, with the UK Experience and other organisations to raise the profile of the Way. The partnership with Walking World is particularly useful as it enables contributors to walk and log routes and raise revenue for their causes. LetsGoNorth has been submitting walks to Walking World for many years.

Public Services

The Highland Council

The first encounter with THC was through the tourism coordinator Colin Simpson whose view was that LetsGoNorth "would be sued" if they tried to go ahead with the project. LetsGoNorth pointed out that Colin did in fact have walks listed on Walking World. LetsGoNorth persevered and eventually a meeting with the North Highland Initiative was set up in November 2013. It was agreed that a community consultancy document would be done. LetsGoNorth wrote the brief (see Annex 2), the Highland Council were adamant that they did. LetsGoNorth were not able to be paid for any work at all stated the Director of Planning and Infrastructure, Stuart

© 2015 Brough Bay Ltd.
All Rights Reserved

Black, as did Colin Simpson. The CEO of THC stated otherwise. It was too late – another contractor was brought in to pull the document together on a paid basis, despite the fact that he did not even know the consultees and LetsGoNorth did.

NHI backed out. They would not want to be party to an argument between LetsGoNorth and THC when they are funded by them.

THC insist that a feasibility study and business plan be drawn up. They do not say how this will be paid for. They have refused funds. They have said that HIE will assess the said documents. LetsGoNorth's voluntary sector arm, the Dunnet Head Educational Trust, asked HIE if they would fund an event which was designed to raise funds for the North Highland Way. HIE said that they would look at a business plan. A draft was written and submitted. HIE said it should be rolled in with the main project and refused to even discuss it. HIE then stated that they wanted the feasibility study and business plan. LetsGoNorth refused to provide it as HIE already stated that no funds would be forthcoming.

Business Gateway

Business Gateway is a partnership of the Highland Council and HIE. LetsGoNorth were told that they had to turn over £70,000 in the first year before they could receive any assistance from HIE and become a managed account. There are many

© 2015 Brough Bay Ltd.
All Rights Reserved

businesses in the Highlands which have been funded by HIE who have earned a lot less.

Scottish Natural Heritage

SNH have always been supportive and continue dialogue with LetsGoNorth with a view to eventually including the Peatlands project under the banner of being within 10 miles of the coast.
VisitScotland

VisitScotland were initially supportive, but when problems arose between the Highland Council and the promoters, they withdrew their support.

They did in fact offer the promoters the opportunity of doing a presentation, which was taken up and well received (October 2013).

They said they would promote the Way on their web sites, but this offer was also withdrawn.

Forestry Commission

Wanted a map showing entry and exit points, but did not want to pay for it. There has been no interaction since.

Community Councils

© 2015 Brough Bay Ltd.
All Rights Reserved

There has been a mixed response. The Durness Community Council initially provided a letter of support but then withdrew it when HIE got involved. Caithness West Community Council provided a letter of support. The full list is available within the feasibility study and business plan.

Private Sector

Dounreay

Dounreay want to see the project practically finished before they will commit anything. They want the feasibility study, business plan and land consultation document. There is no indication of how these are going to be paid for.

The participating businesses

Several of the businesses indicted that they had had an increase in bookings since the launch of the Way. The most vociferous of these was the Ben Loyal Hotel in Tongue

Updates

There is updated information available at the news service at www.letsgonorthnewsservice.com. There is a subscription fee of £15 to pay. On the site is all the correspondence with public services and other organisations. Some businessmen were not really businessmen and wanted everything done for free and

© 2015 Brough Bay Ltd.
All Rights Reserved

even be given products free of charge. In general though the businesses

Recommendations

That whoever purchases the feasibility study and business plan should look for funding. The land owner consultation is being worked on as this document is being written.

© 2015 Brough Bay Ltd.
All Rights Reserved

Annex 1

Telephone Consultation on the concept of a North Highland Way by Bill Taylor Associates
January 2014

Final report on telephone consultation on the concept of a North Highland Way
by Bill Taylor Associates
On behalf of Highland Council
January 2014
Introduction

Introduction

The idea of a North Highland Way which would run from John o Groats to Cape Wrath has been around for some time. Recently a local company has undertaken some work to explore the concept further and has involved a number of local businesses. A meeting between The Highland Council the North Highland Initiative (NHI) and the company agreed that the idea had great potential for the area but neither the Council nor NHI were currently in a position to lead such a project. Similarly the company indicated that they were not in a position to continue

© 2015 Brough Bay Ltd.
All Rights Reserved

undertaking the level of work that would be required if this was on a voluntary basis. A petition indicated a degree of interest from local residents and visitors to the area.

Since the creation of a statutory right of responsible access in 2003 there is no longer a need for the public sector in Scotland to designate national long distance routes to provide a guaranteed right of access. However many communities see the potential for economic benefit from having a designated route in their area with a number of routes already successfully created by local community and / or tourism groups. In the Highland area this includes the South Loch Ness Trail. A further project is taking this approach to the development of the Cape Wrath Trail. It is envisaged that this approach may be an appropriate one for the North Highland Way. Such a route would link in with the Cape Wrath Trail in the west and the Moray Firth Trail in the east.

The Highland Council commissioned Bill Taylor Associates to undertake of a short piece of work to gauge the level of community interest in the formation of a group to take forward the development of a North Highland Way long distance walking route.

This report outlines the findings of this exercise.

Methodology
Telephone contact was made with a range of organisation and individuals supplied by Highland

© 2015 Brough Bay Ltd.
All Rights Reserved

Council. Calls were made between 18th December and 21st January. Several of the contacts required many calls before a successful interview was possible. This was undoubtedly due to the timing of the exercise.

The following organisations, groups and agencies were contacted (full list Appendix 1):

? 11 Chairpersons of Community Councils along the North coast
? 2 Community Development Companies
? 3 Regional scale development organisations
? 1 local tourism development group

© 2015 Brough Bay Ltd.
All Rights Reserved

ANNEX 2

NORTH HIGHLAND WAY COMMUNITY CONSULTATION SPECIFICATION

SUMMARY

The Highland Council wish to commission the undertaking of a short piece of work to gauge the level of community interest in the formation of a group to take forward the development of a North Highland Way long distance walking route which could incorporate facilities similar to those found on the South West Coastal path. The proposed route is from John o' Groats, linking in with the Moray Firth Trail, to Cape Wrath, linking in with the Cape Wrath Trail.

BACKGROUND

© 2015 Brough Bay Ltd.
All Rights Reserved

The idea of a North Highland Way that would run from Cape Wrath to John o' Groats has been around for some time and more recently a local company Brough Bay Ltd has undertaken some work to explore the concept further and has involved a number of local businesses. At a recent meeting between The Highland Council the North Highland Initiative (NHI) and Brough Bay Ltd all parties agreed that the idea had great potential for the area but neither the Council nor NHI were currently in a position to lead such a project. Similarly Brough Bay Ltd indicated that they were not in a position to continue undertaking the level of work that would be required if this was on a voluntary basis. A petition has also indicated a degree of interest in the project from both local residents and visitors to the area.

Since the Land Reform Act created a statutory right of responsible access in 2003 there is no longer a need for the public sector in Scotland to designate national long distance routes to provide a guaranteed right of access. However many communities see the potential for

© 2015 Brough Bay Ltd.
All Rights Reserved

economic benefit from having a designated route in their area with a number of routes already successfully created by local community and / or tourism groups. In the Highland area this includes the South Loch Ness Trail while a further project under way at present is taking this approach to the development of the Cape Wrath Trail. It is envisaged that this approach may also be an appropriate one for the North Highland Way

REQUIRED OUTCOME

Recognising that the project cannot move forward without a lead organisation the Highland Council has agreed to fund a short piece of work to be undertaken independently to gauge the level of support for the idea and to what extent potential stakeholders could be involved in taking such a project forward. The geography of the area, time of year, travel issues and the need to involve organisations that often rely of volunteers mean it is not practical to do this by holding a meeting but instead initial interest will be gauged through a series of telephone interviews.

A range of stakeholders will require to be interviewed as detailed in the table overleaf. Each interview undertaken should include a short piece of background as to why contact has been made and should be followed by questions to ascertain the following:-

- Is the organisation already aware of any proposal to develop a North Highland Way?
- Does the organisation support the principle of a North Highland Way?
- Do they see this as being an initiative that could be community led?
- If a community led group was set up to develop the route what level of support could the organisation give? The consultant should ensure so far as is possible whether commitments might be in time, expertise, financial or in other forms.
- Do they have any other observations on

the proposal to develop a North Highland Way?

Responses to all interviews must be recorded and retained.

List of interviewees to be contacted under this contract

Community Councils

Bettyhill, Strathnaver & Altnaharra
Bower

© 2015 Brough Bay Ltd.
All Rights Reserved

Caithness West

Castletown

Dunnet and Canisbay

Durness

Halkirk

Melvich

Strathy & Armadale

Thurso

Tongue

© 2015 Brough Bay Ltd.
All Rights Reserved

Other community Organisations

Durness Development Group

Melness Development Group

Moray Firth Partnership

RSPB Dunnet Head

Caithness Waybaggers

© 2015 Brough Bay Ltd.
All Rights Reserved

Public sector organisations

The Highland Council

Scottish Natural Heritage

Forestry Commission Scotland

Highlands & Islands Enterprise

VisitScotland

© 2015 Brough Bay Ltd.
All Rights Reserved

Private sector businesses and organisations

Brough Bay Ltd

North Highland Initiative

TIMESCALE AND SUBMISSION OF PROPOSALS

© 2015 Brough Bay Ltd.
All Rights Reserved

A short report detailing who was interviewed and giving a brief summary of their response should be submitted following completion of the interviews. A provisional date for this is by Friday 24th January 2014 but this date may be varied with the agreement of the Council to allow for elements such as fitting in with community council meeting schedules. The report should be delivered for the attention of:

Colin Simpson

Tourism Co-ordinator

The Highland Council

Glenurquhart Road

Inverness

IV3 5NX

Further enquiries about this brief can be directed to Colin Simpson – Tel: 01463 702957 or e-mail colin.simpson@highland.gov.uk

© 2015 Brough Bay Ltd.
All Rights Reserved

© 2015 Brough Bay Ltd.
All Rights Reserved

© 2015 Brough Bay Ltd.
All Rights Reserved

© 2015 Brough Bay Ltd.
All Rights Reserved

© 2015 Brough Bay Ltd.
All Rights Reserved

© 2015 Brough Bay Ltd.
All Rights Reserved

www.ingramcontent.com/pod-product-compliance
Lightning Source LLC
Chambersburg PA
CBHW070434180526
45158CB00017B/1241